TROJAN

BY **KRIS KNIGHT**

ILLUSTRATED BY **JAKE HILL**

Walkthrough

Read this first - or turn the page to go straight to the story!

The Characters

Trent

Trent loves computer games. He is shy - but he has to learn to be brave!

Iris

Iris is a character in Trent's game. She is a good fighter. Can she help Trent?

The Codec

The Codec are a virus. They want to escape the computer. Can Trent stop them?

Key Facts

motherboard

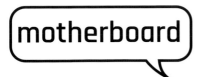

The motherboard controls the computer. Trent has to get there!

The Key is a code Trent needs to find. It will unlock the way out of the game.

The Key

Trojan code

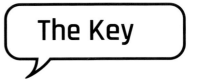

The Trojan code holds the power to reveal the key. Trent must use the Trojan code to stop the Codec.

Story Background

Inside Trent's computer there is a virus called the Codec. They want to escape the computer and infect the outside world. Will Trent be able to stop the Codec?

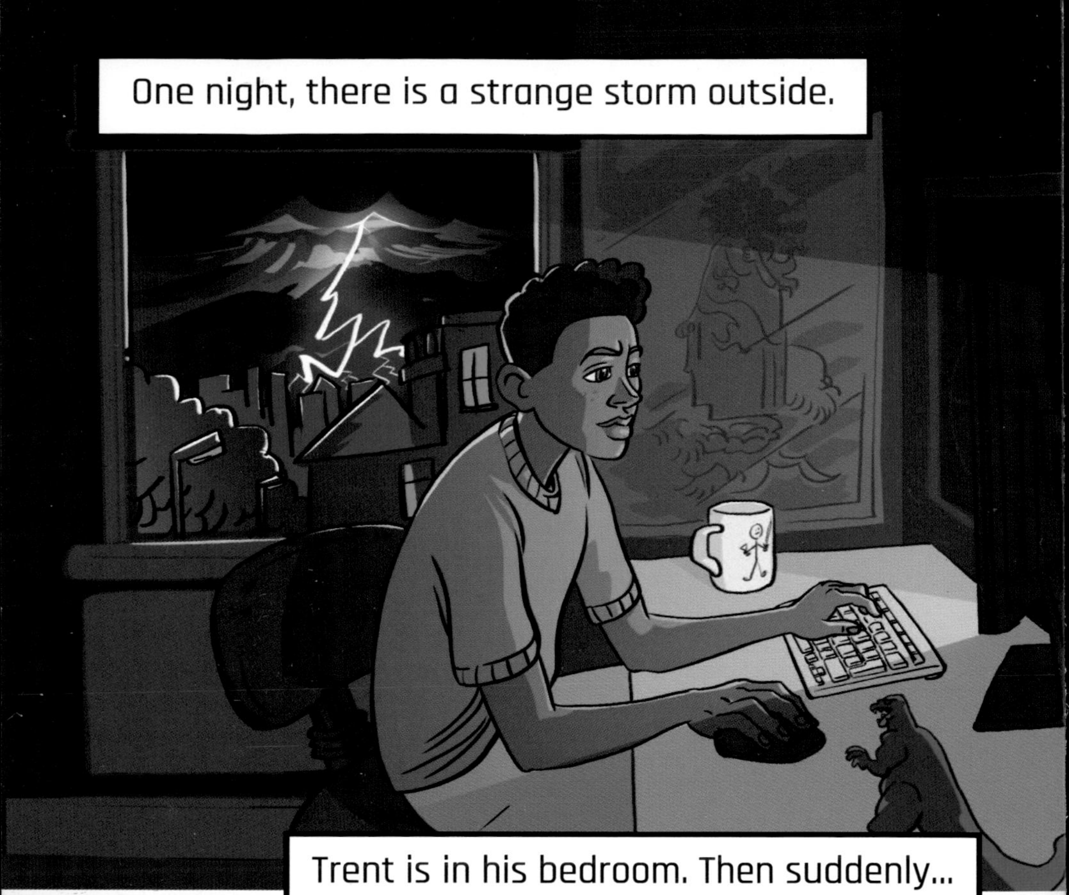
One night, there is a strange storm outside.

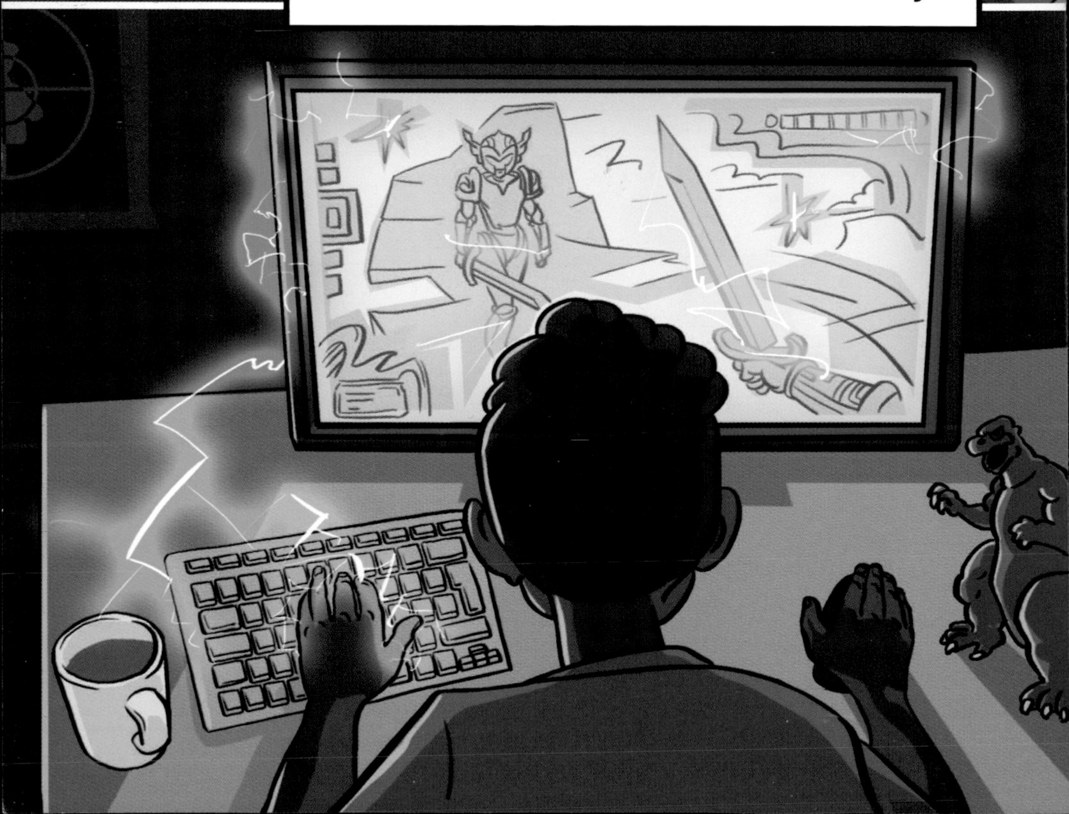
Trent is in his bedroom. Then suddenly...

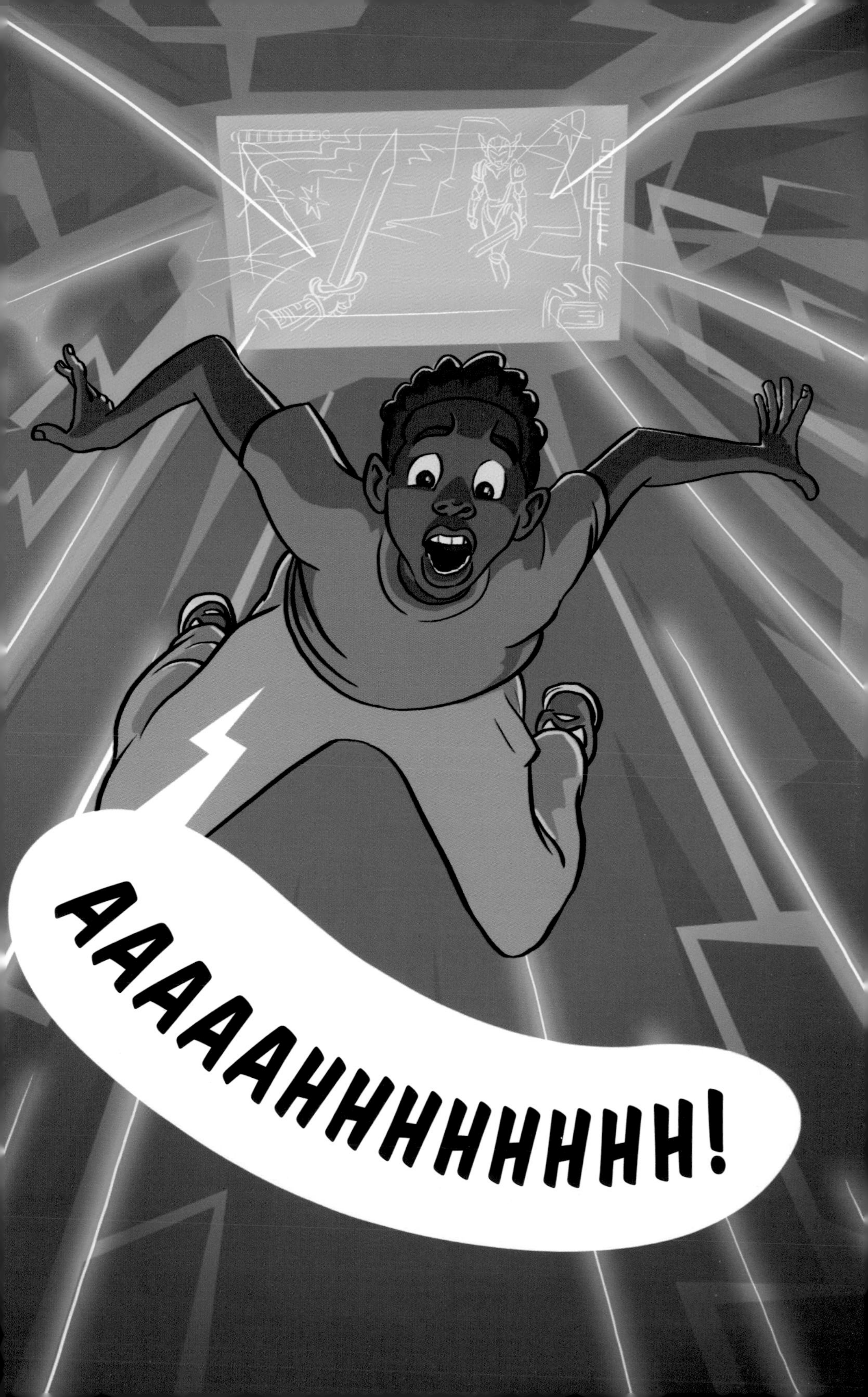
AAAAAHHHHHHHHH!

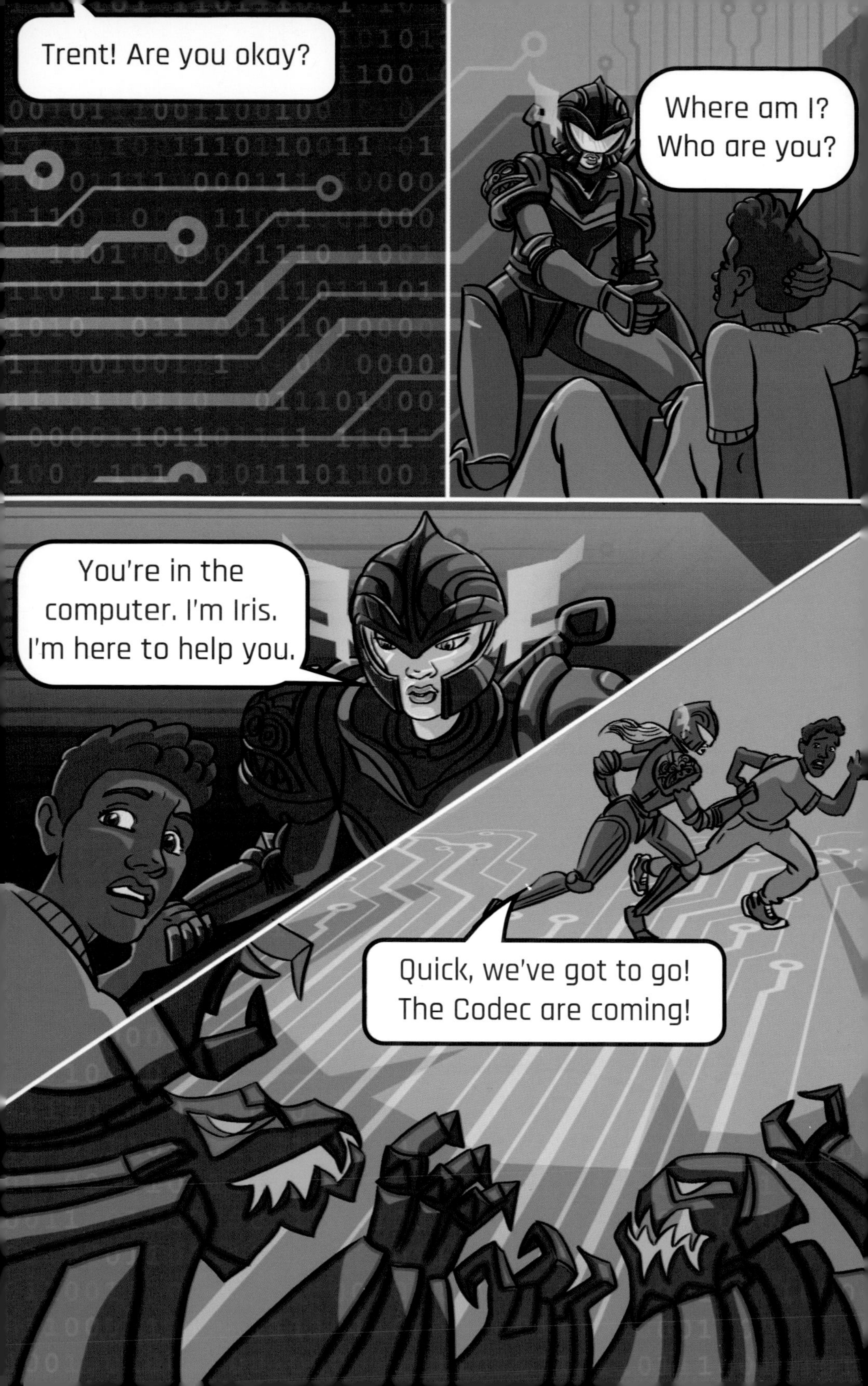
Trent! Are you okay?
Where am I? Who are you?
You're in the computer. I'm Iris. I'm here to help you.
Quick, we've got to go! The Codec are coming!

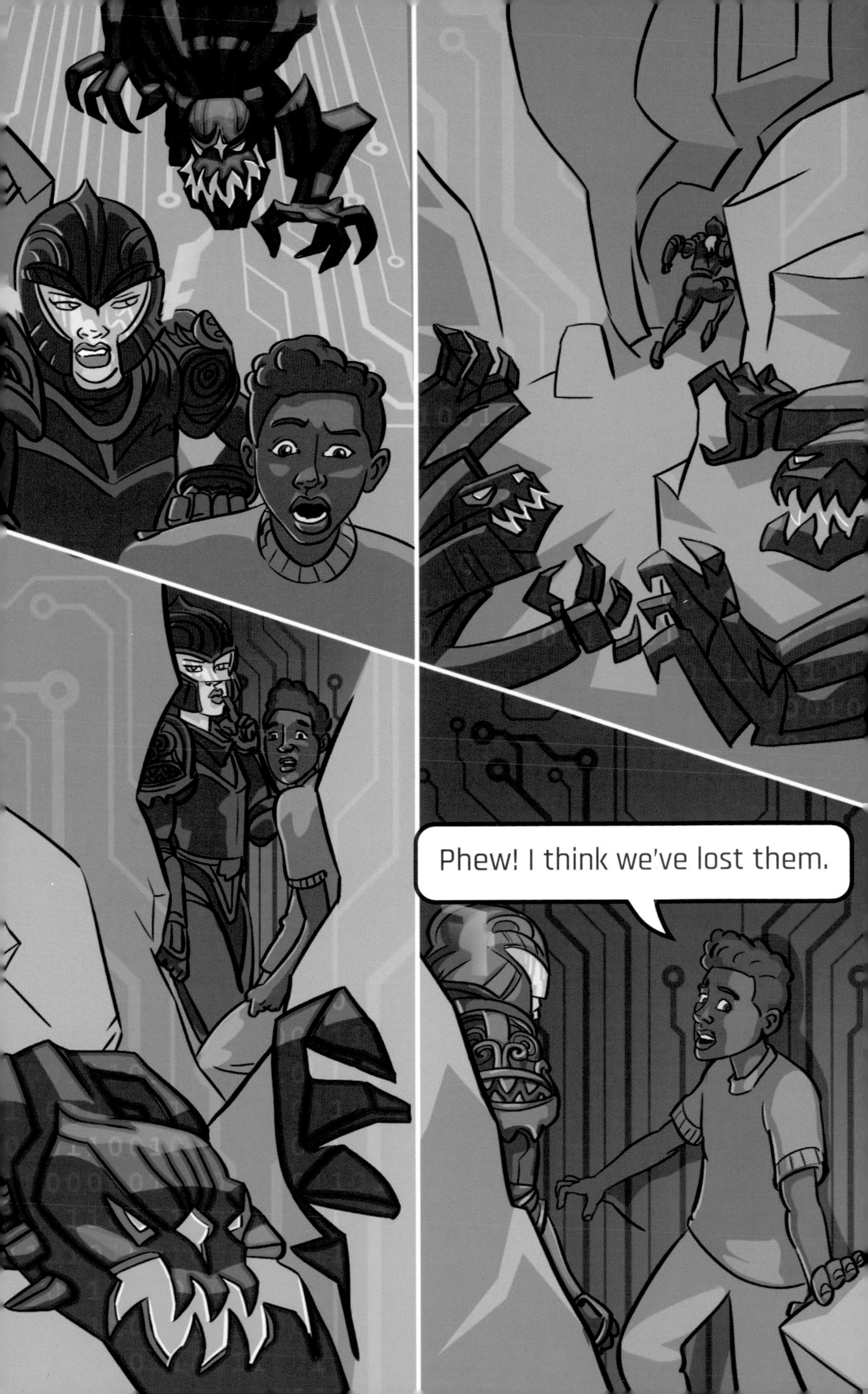
Phew! I think we've lost them.

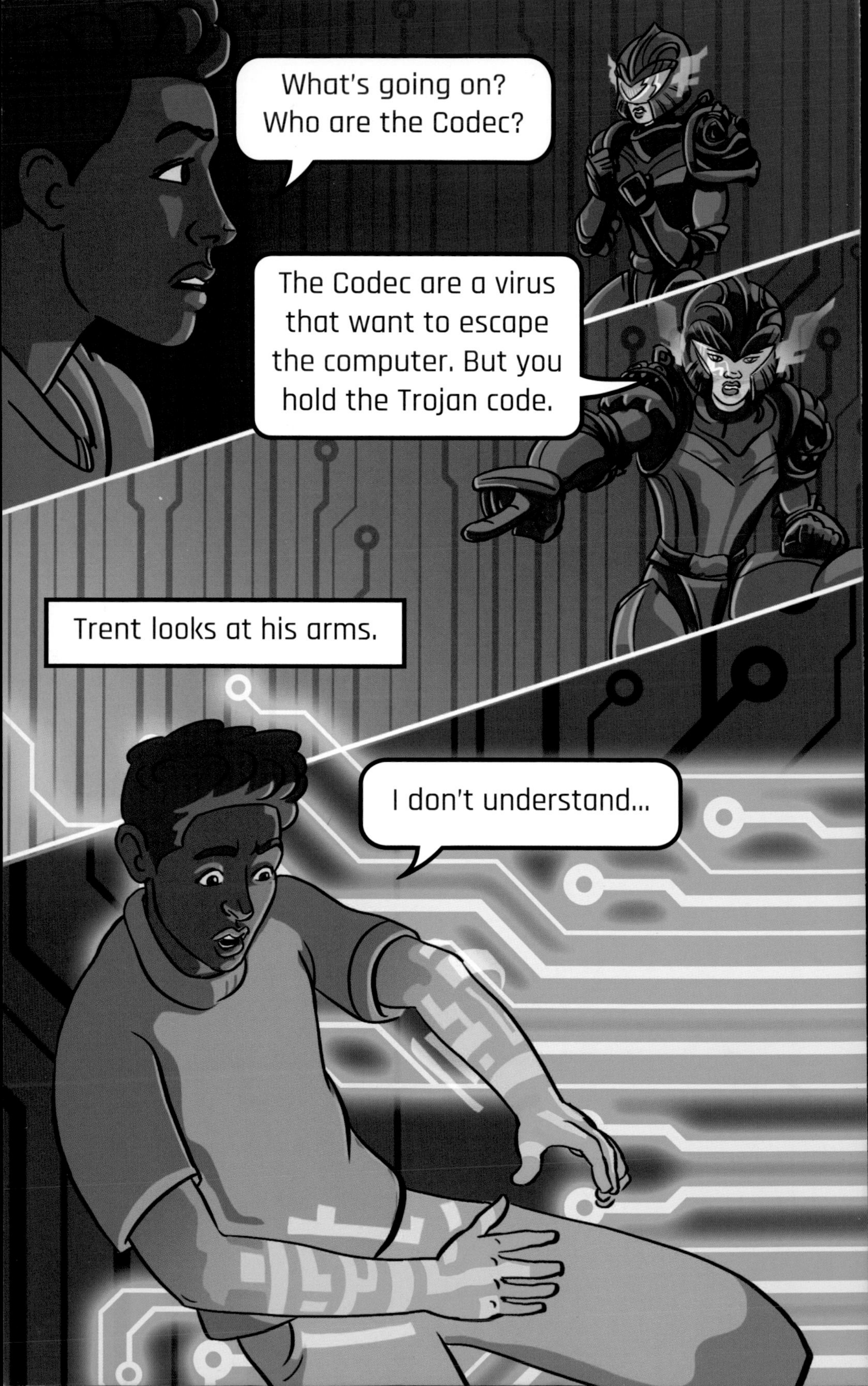
What's going on? Who are the Codec?
The Codec are a virus that want to escape the computer. But you hold the Trojan code.
Trent looks at his arms.
I don't understand...

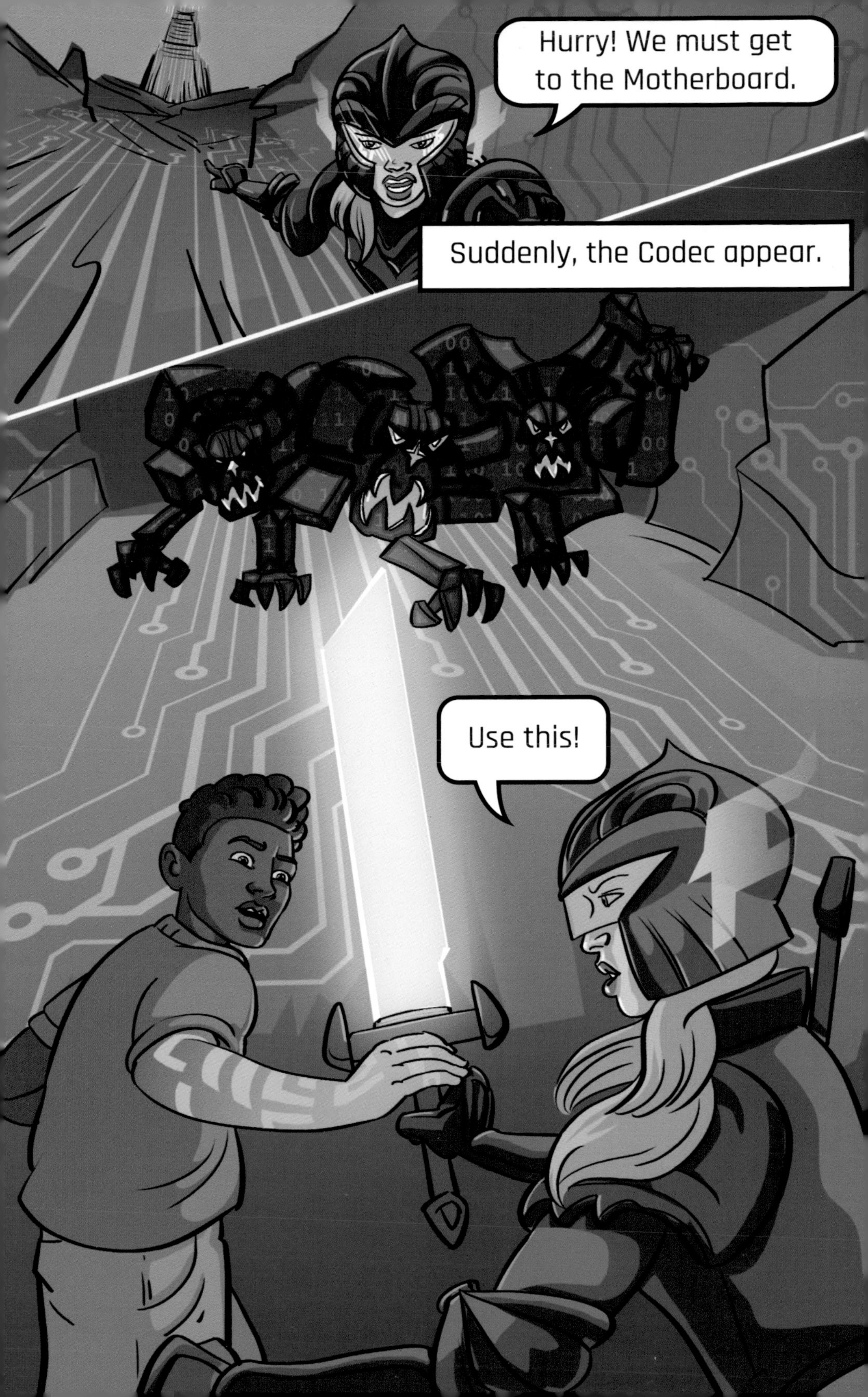
Hurry! We must get to the Motherboard.
Suddenly, the Codec appear.
Use this!

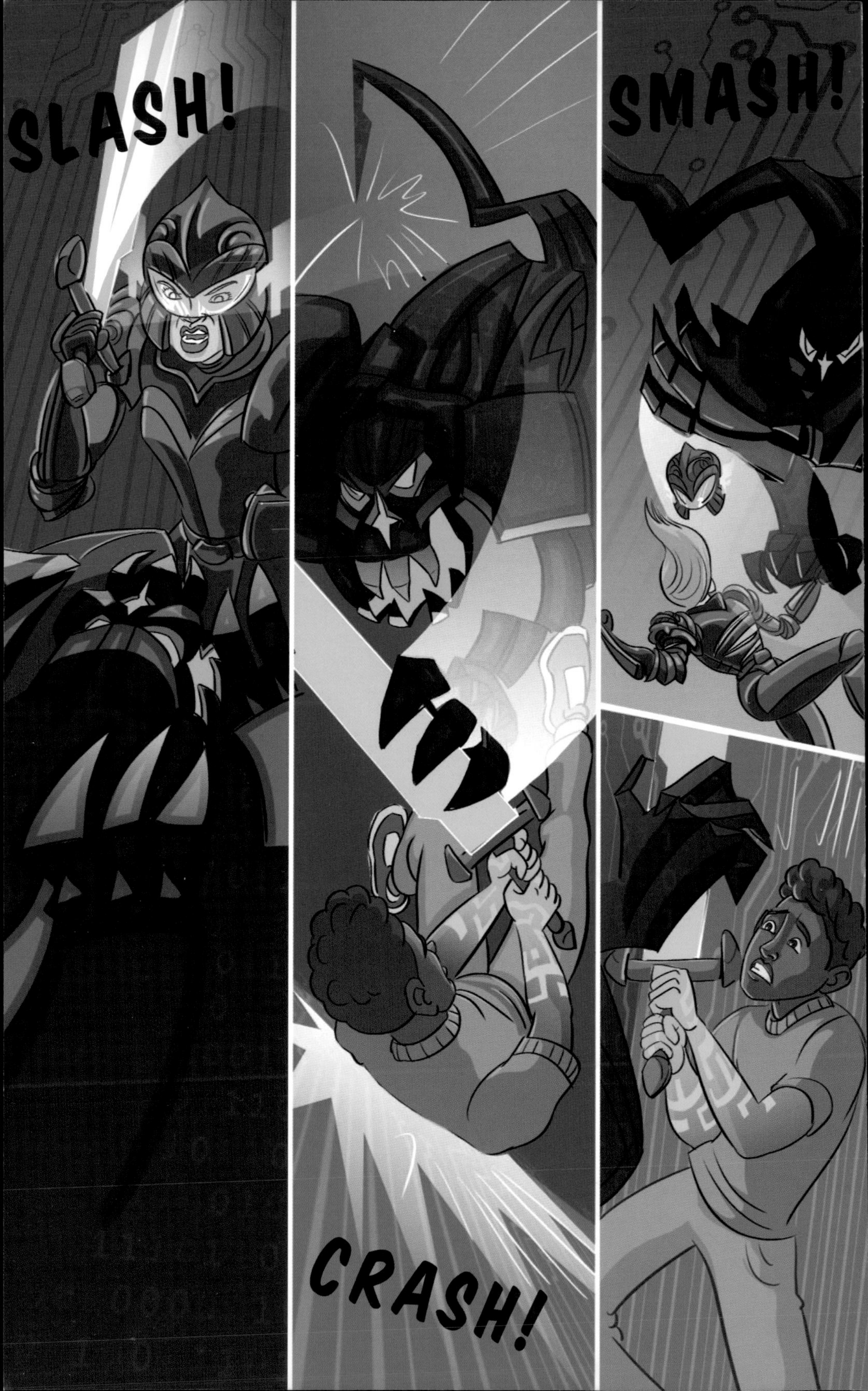
SLASH!
CRASH!
SMASH!

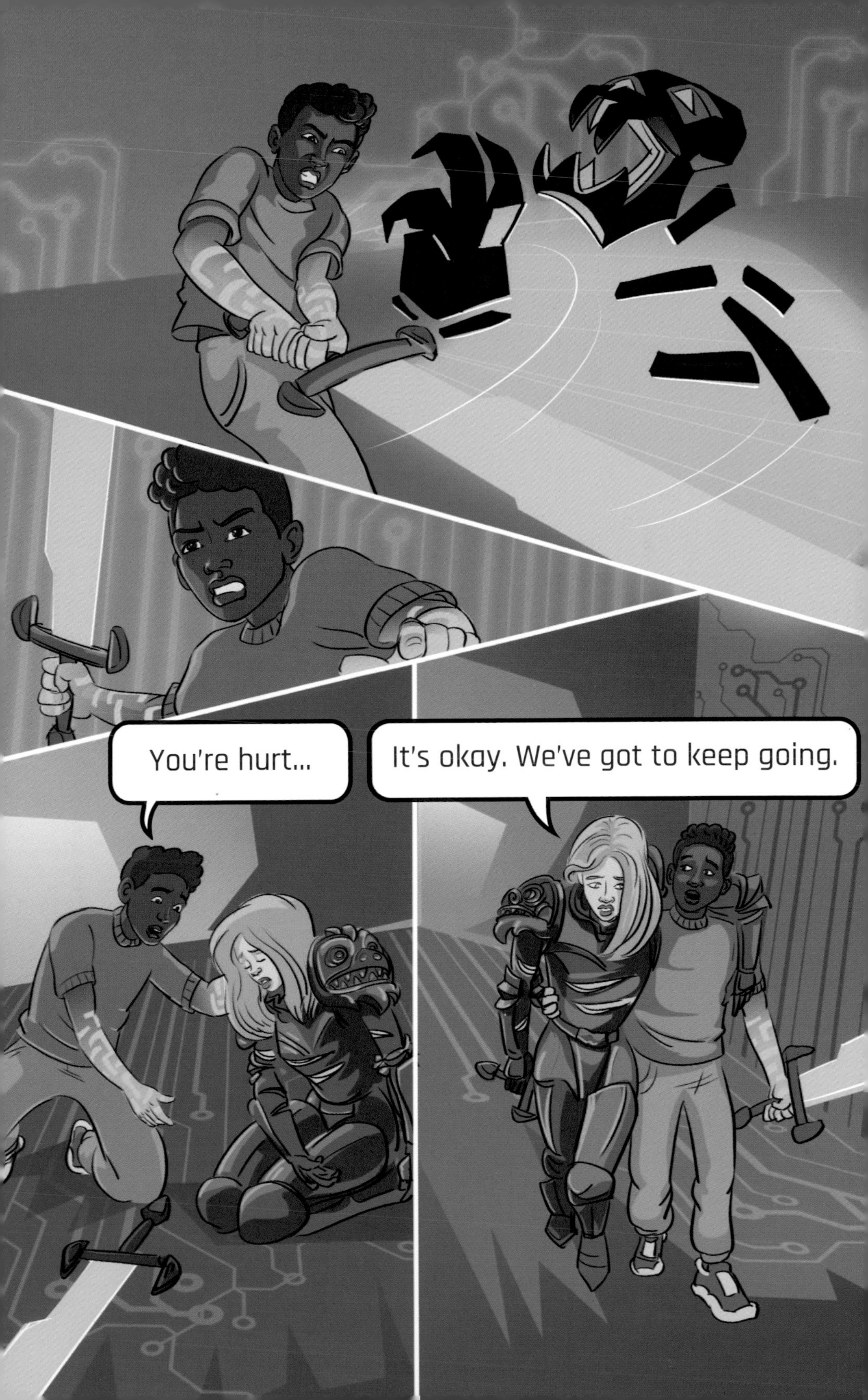
You're hurt...
It's okay. We've got to keep going.

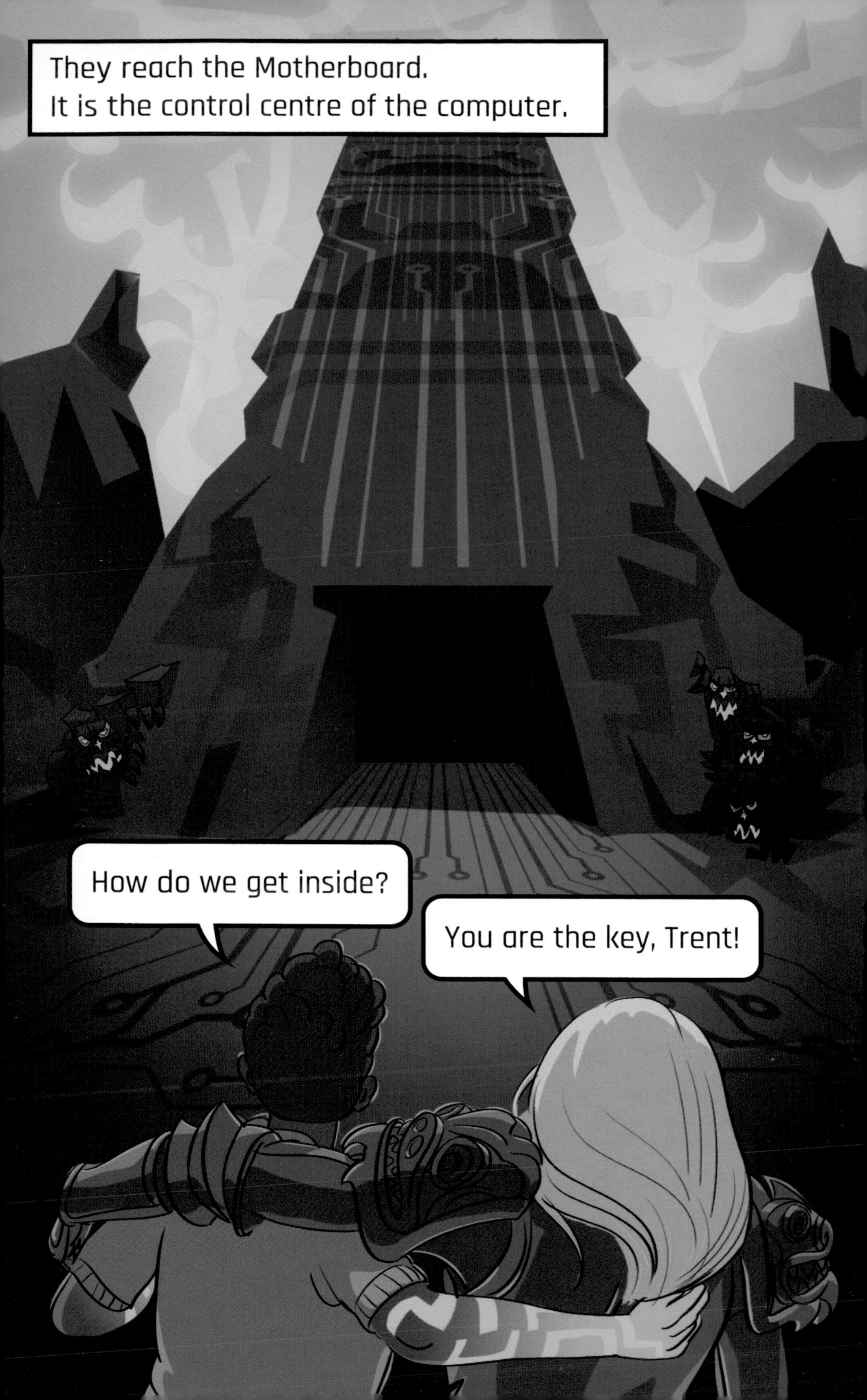
They reach the Motherboard.
It is the control centre of the computer.
How do we get inside?
You are the key, Trent!

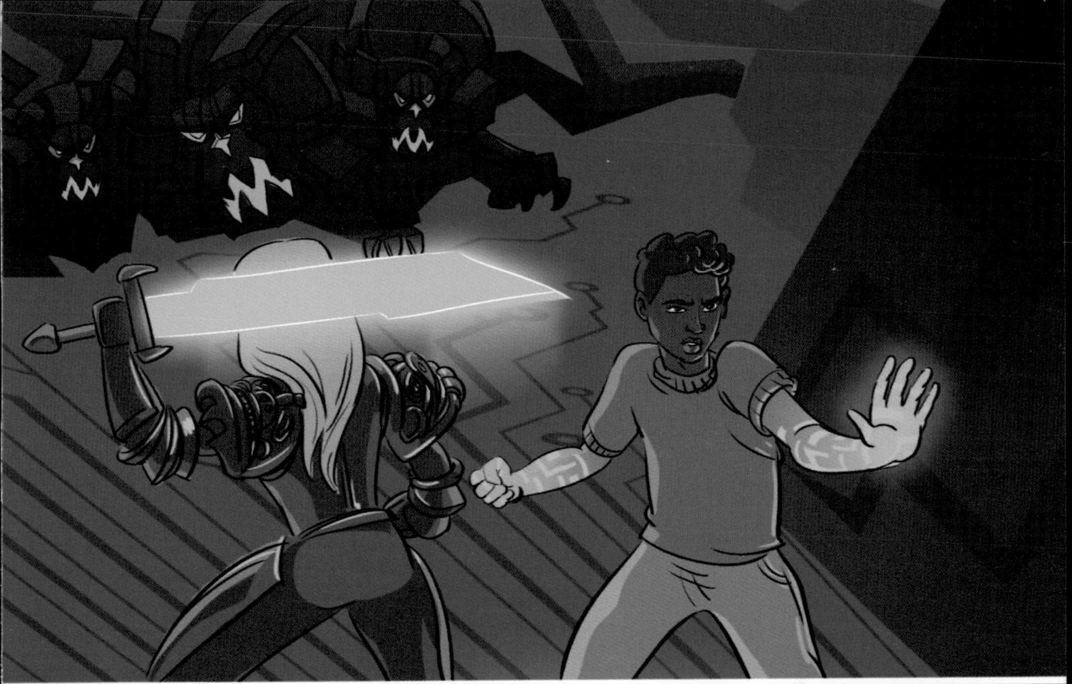

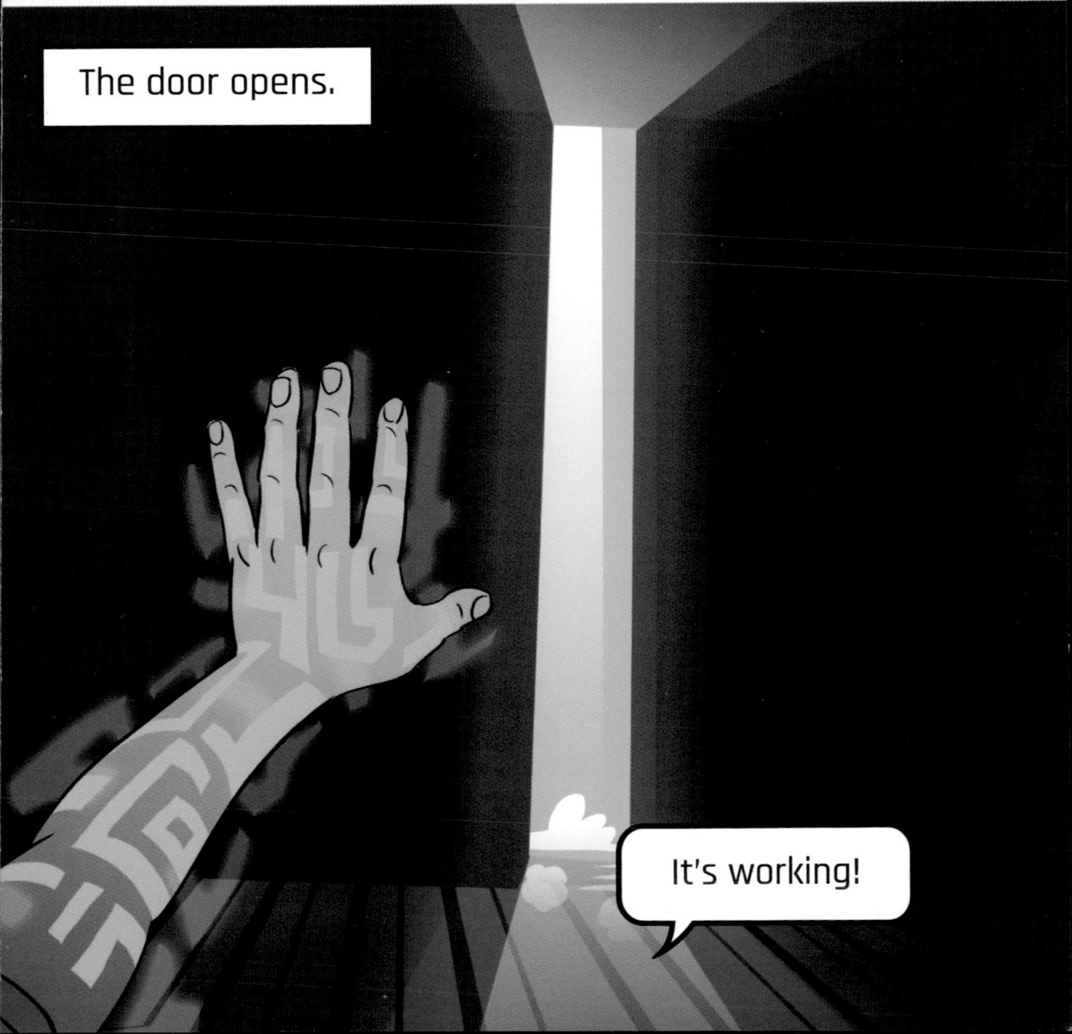
The door opens.
It's working!

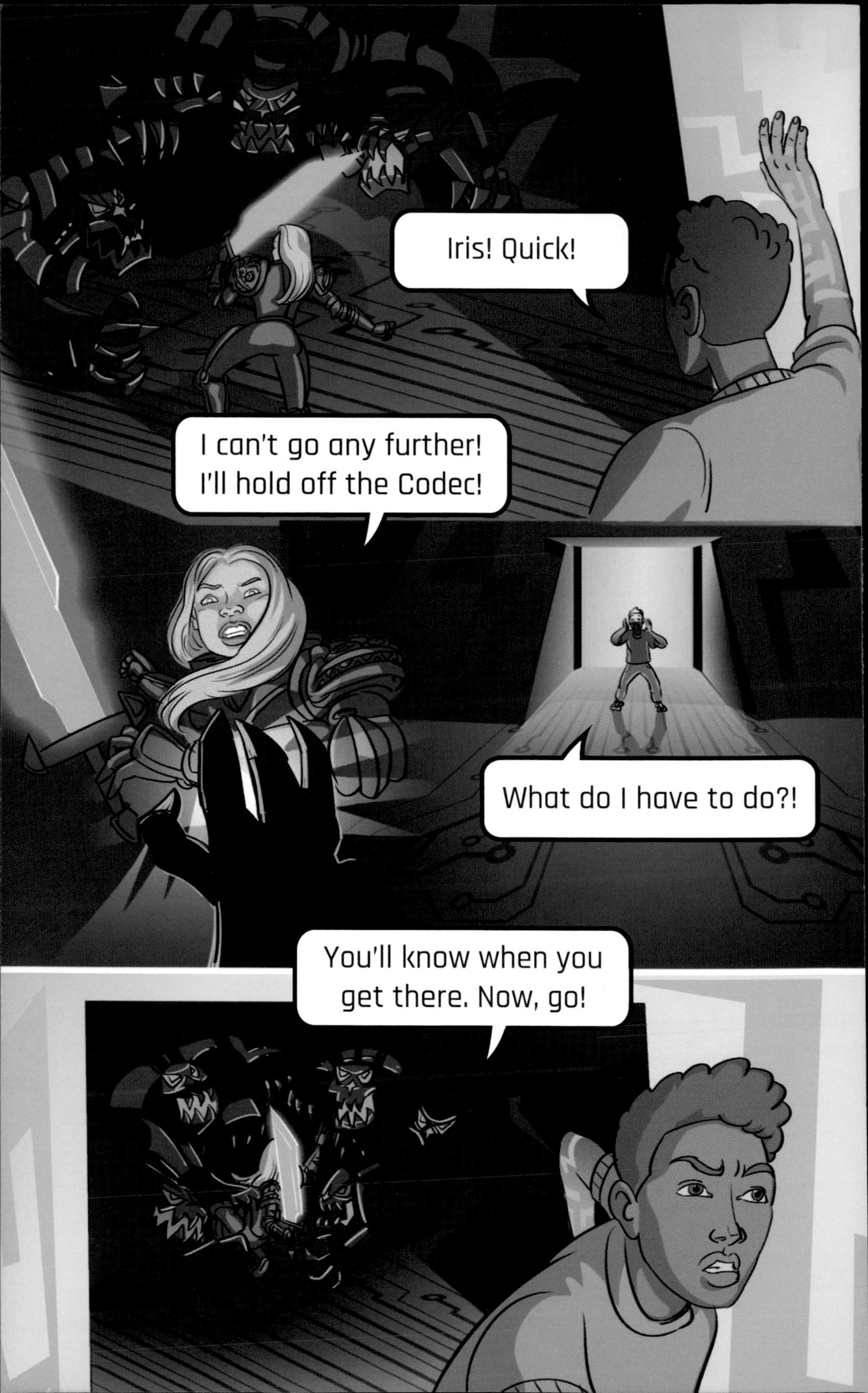
Iris! Quick!
I can't go any further! I'll hold off the Codec!
What do I have to do?!
You'll know when you get there. Now, go!

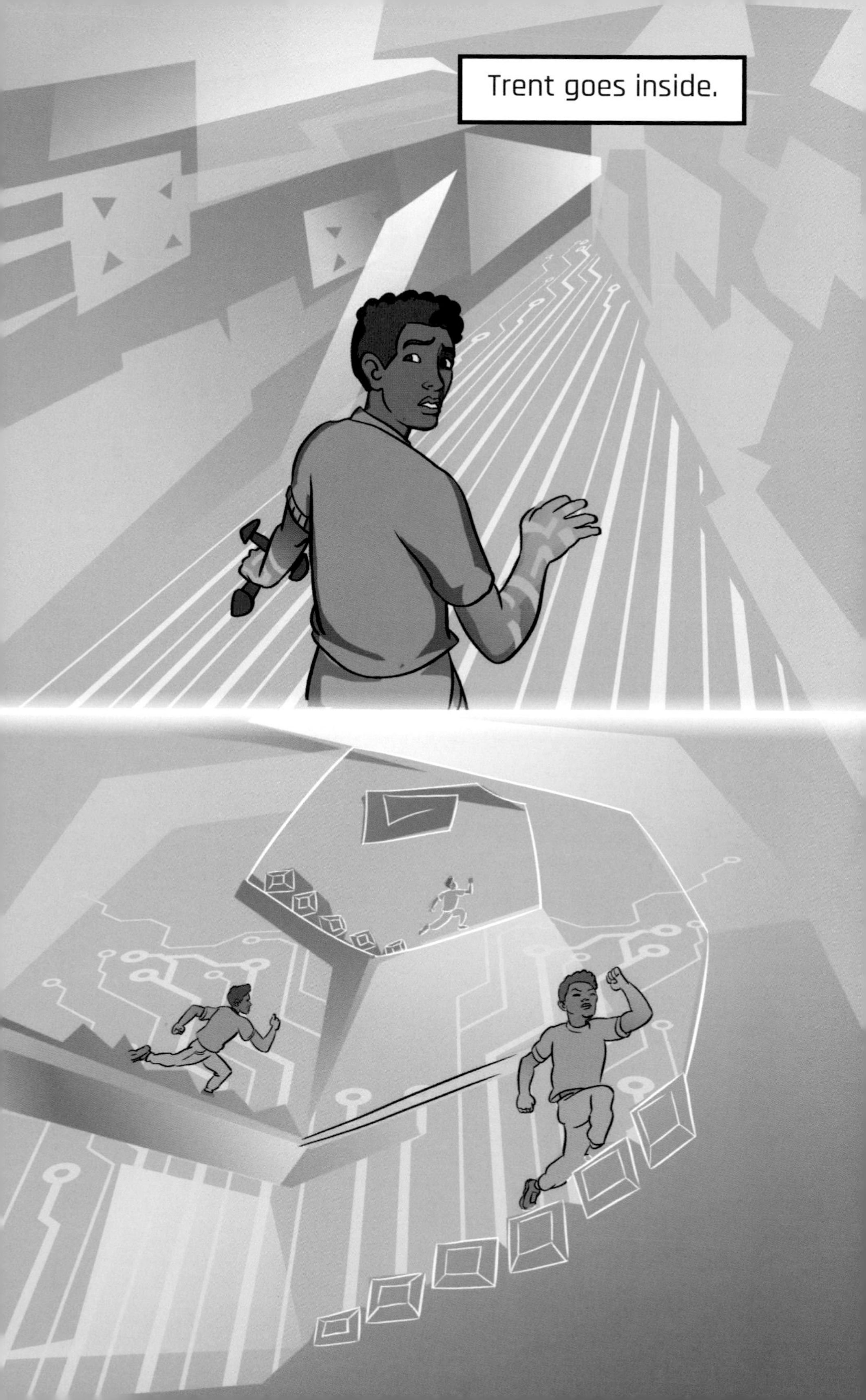
Trent goes inside.

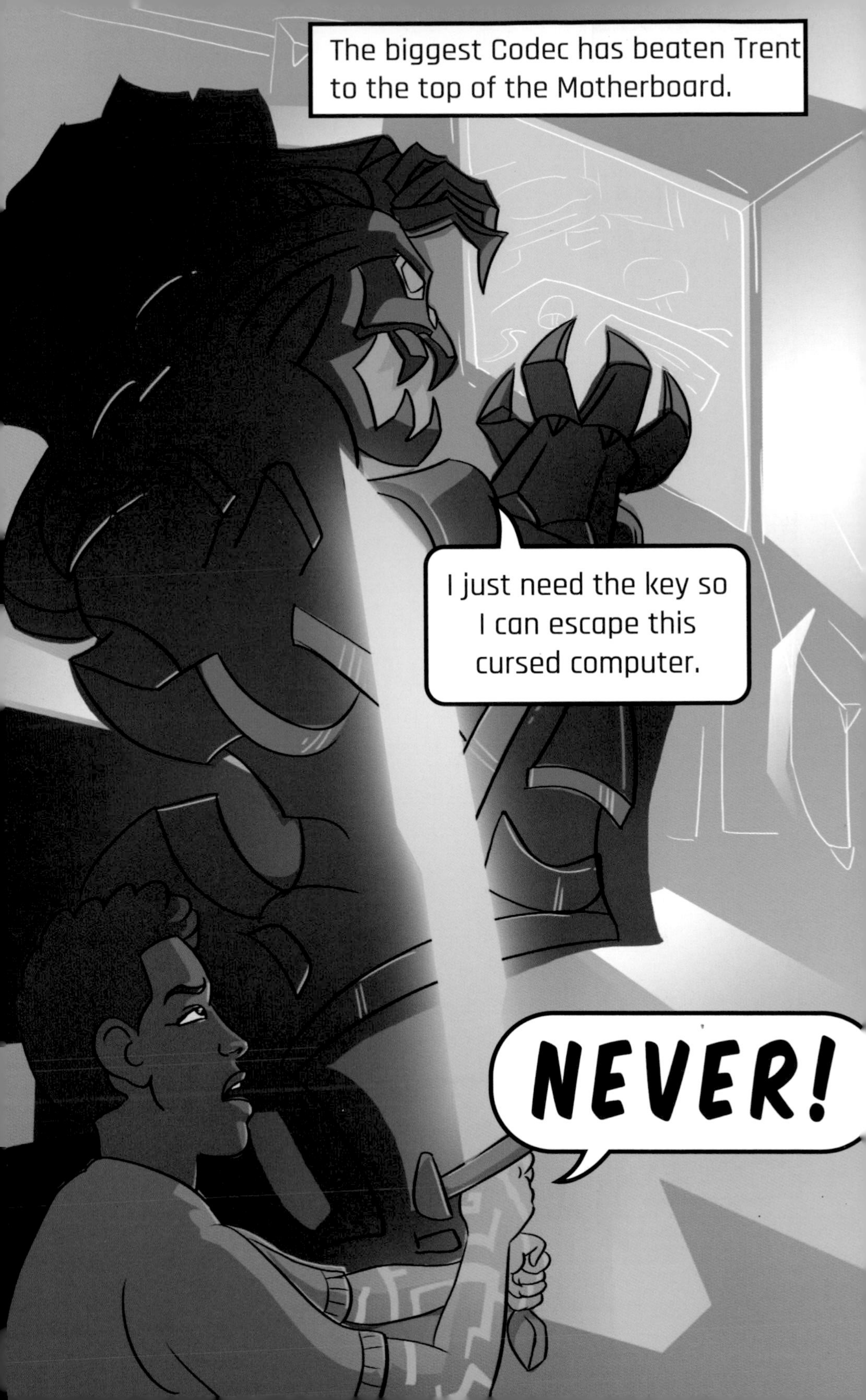
The biggest Codec has beaten Trent to the top of the Motherboard.
I just need the key so I can escape this cursed computer.
NEVER!

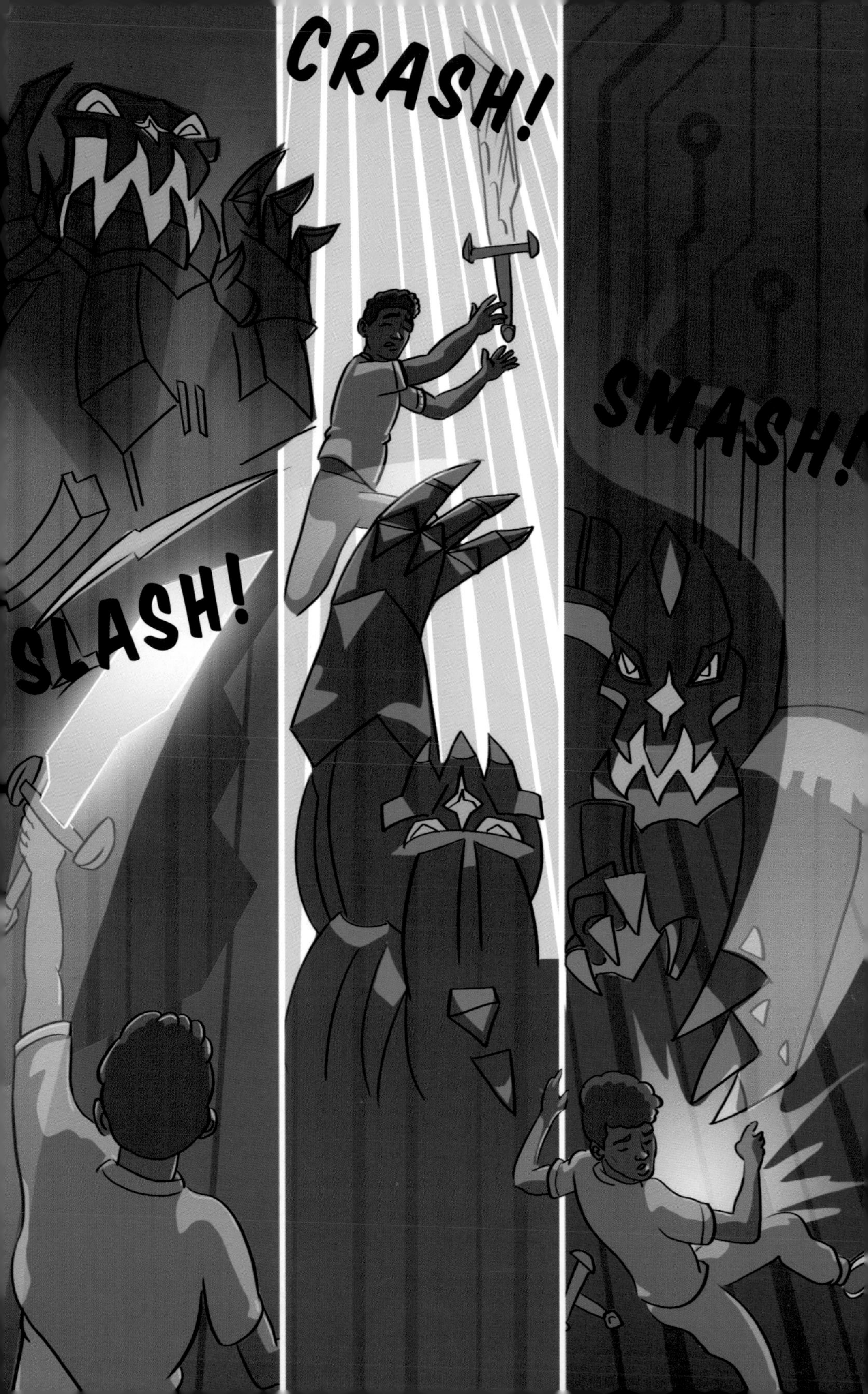

SLASH!
CRASH!
SMASH!

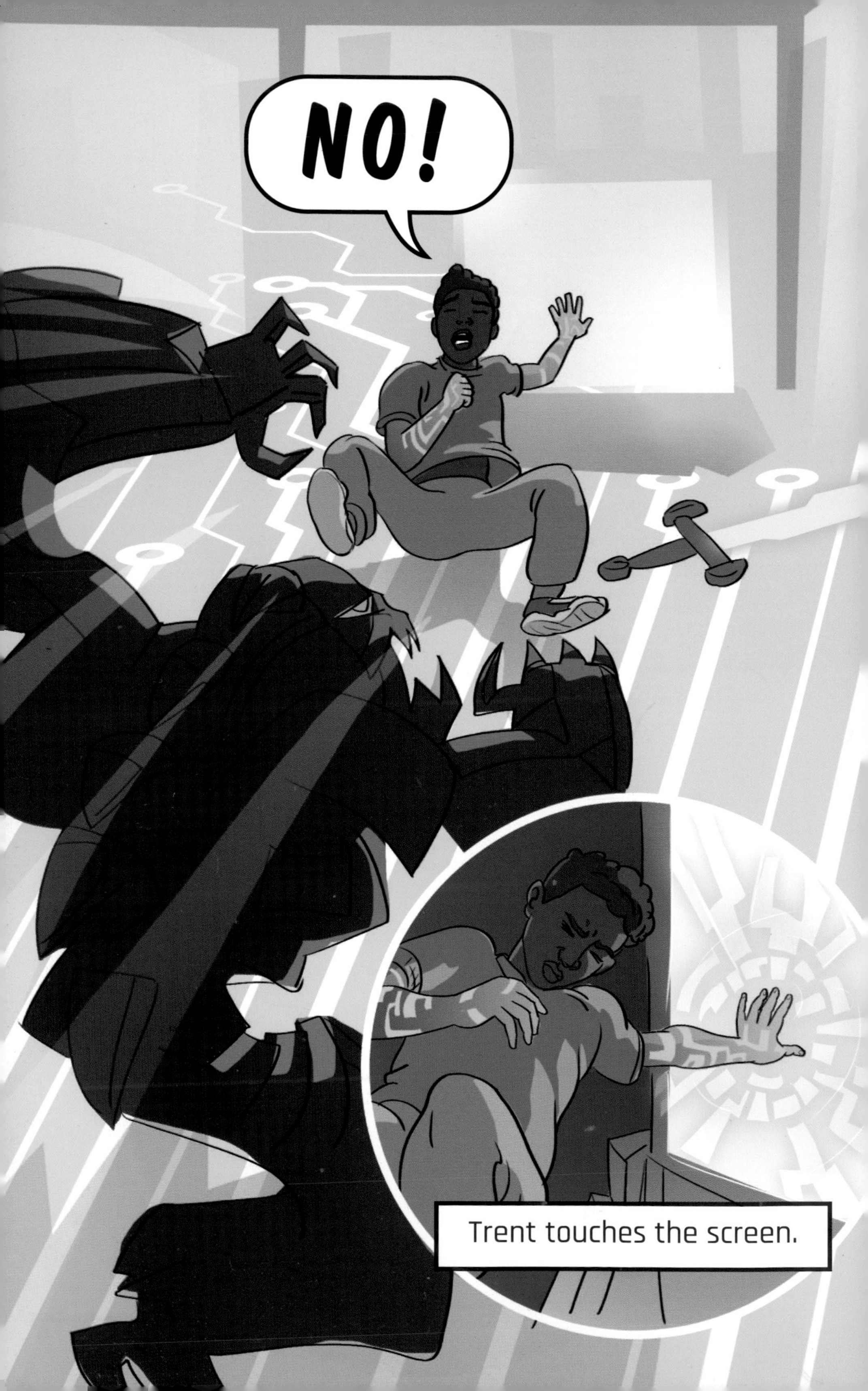
NO!
Trent touches the screen.

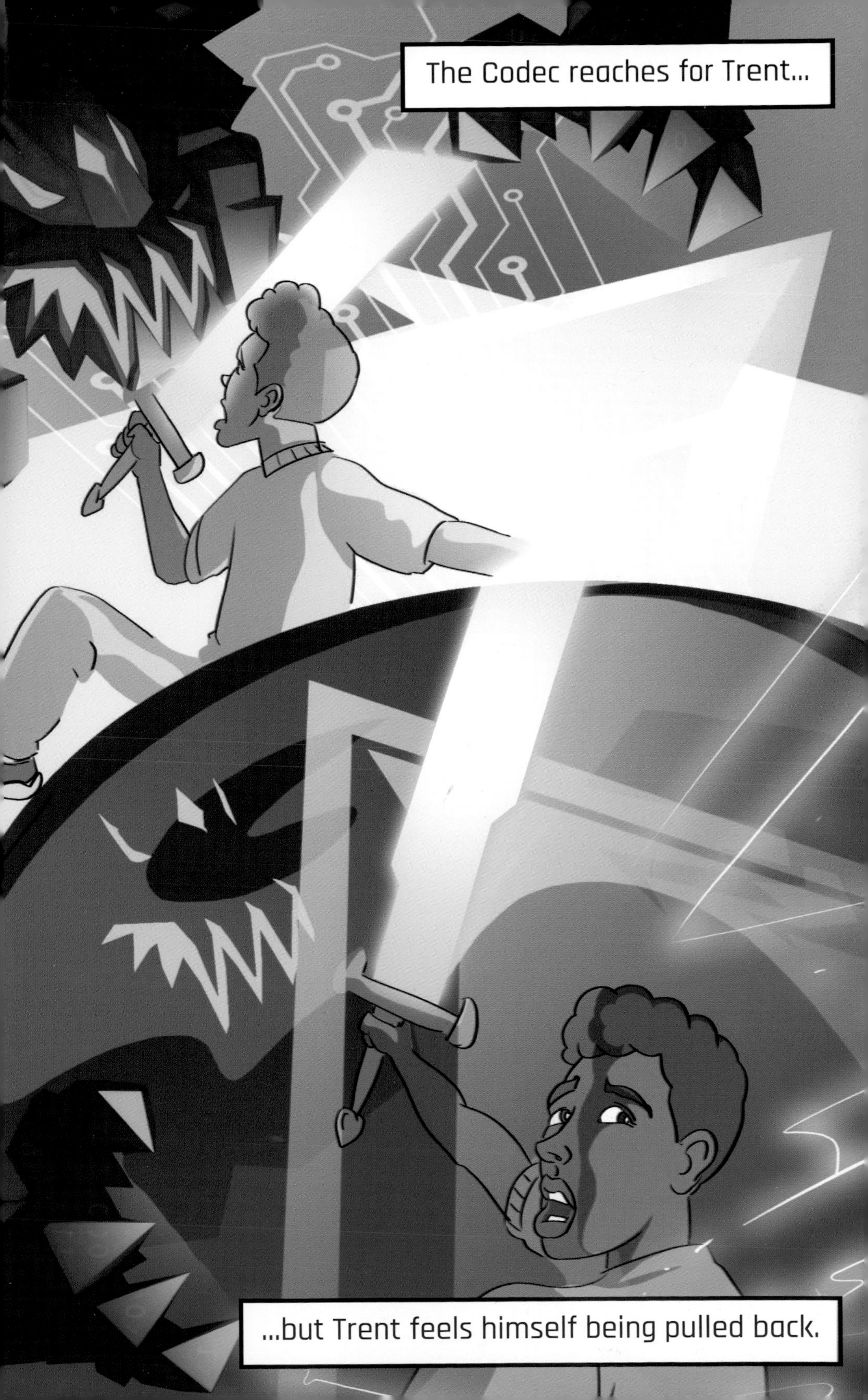
The Codec reaches for Trent...
...but Trent feels himself being pulled back.

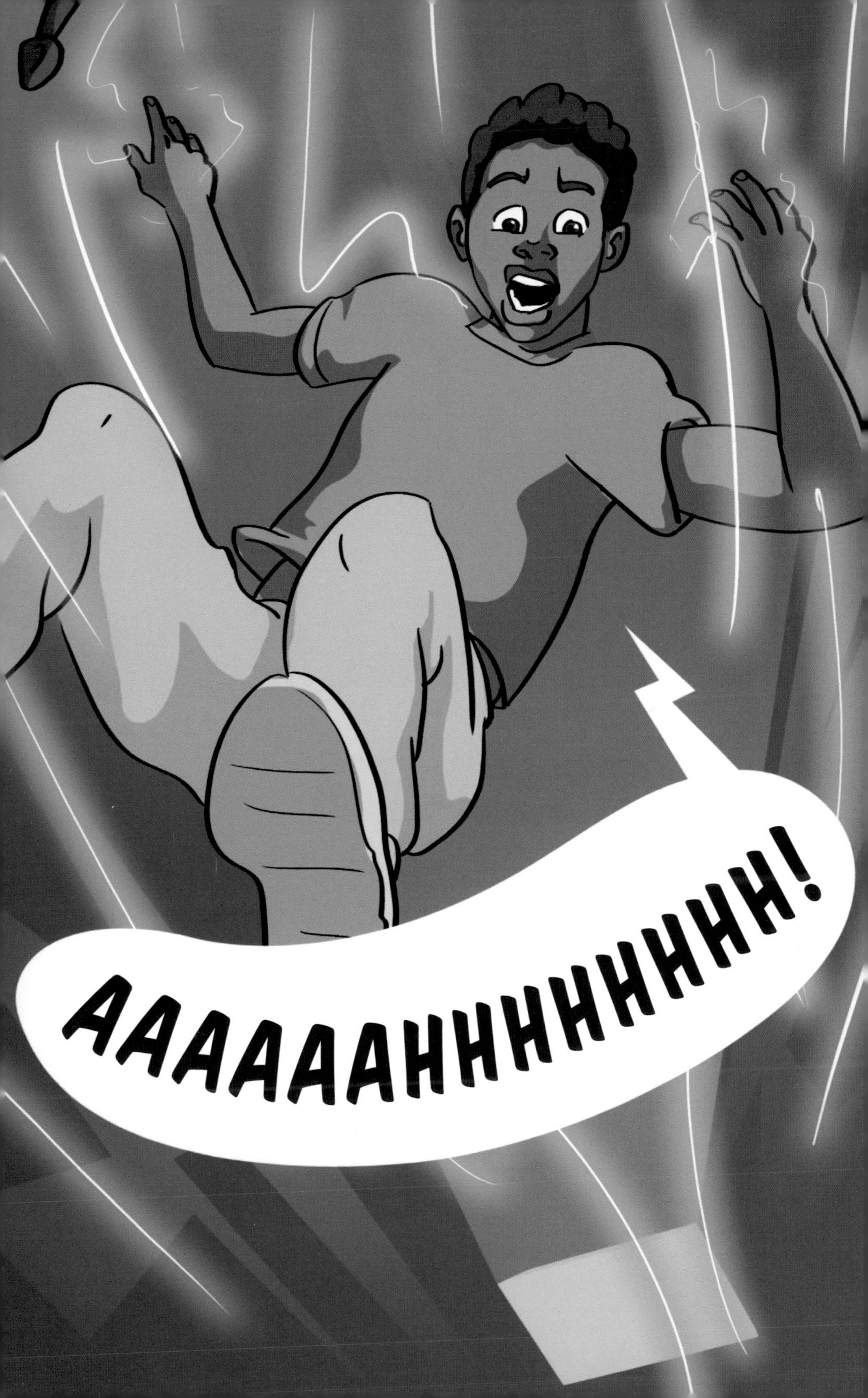
AAAAAAHHHHHHHHH!

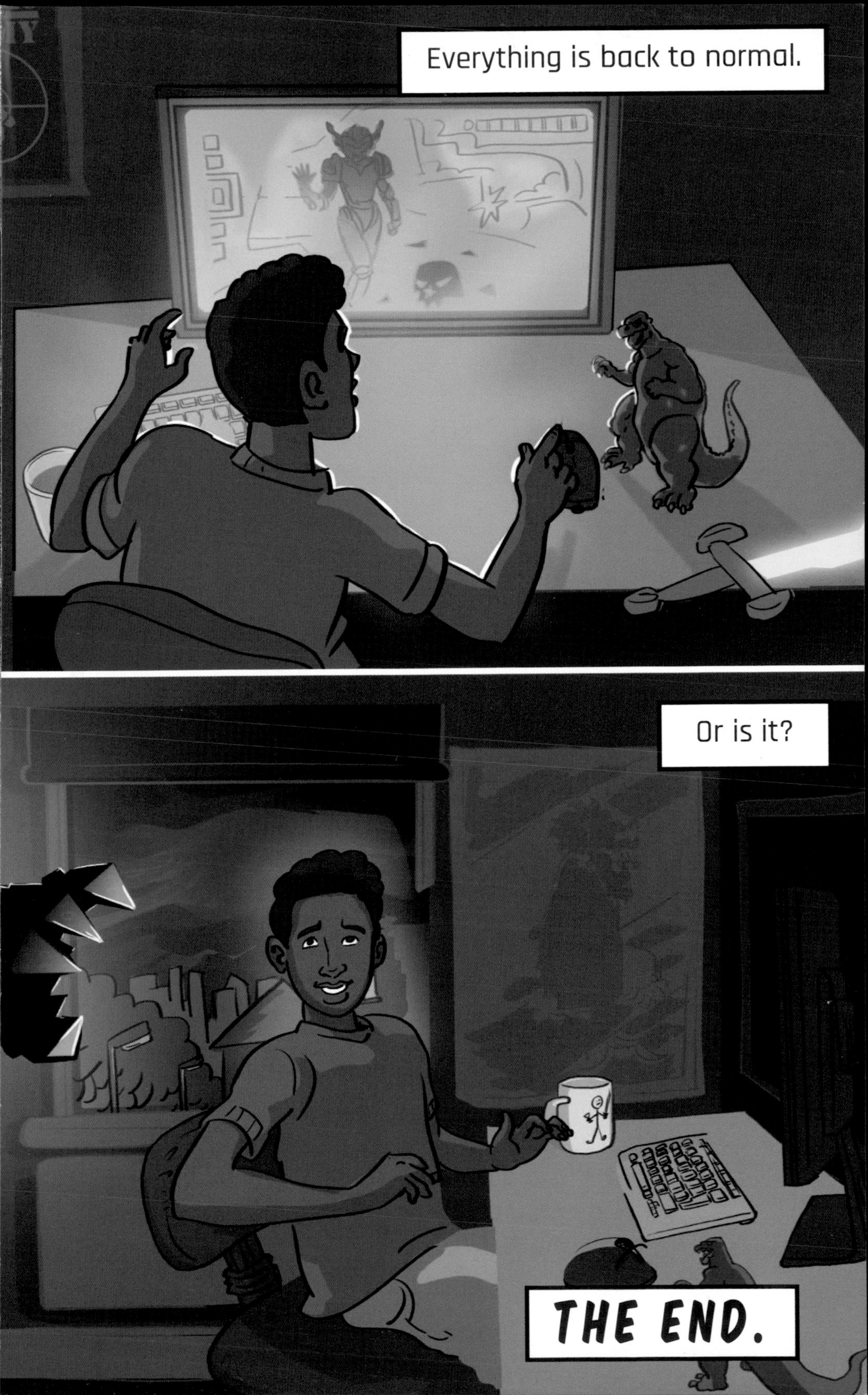
Everything is back to normal.
Or is it?
THE END.

Level Up...

Answer the questions below. Each correct answer gains you points. Are you a Trainee or a Grand Master?

1 *Multiple Choice:*
How does Trent end up in the computer? **1pt**
a) The Codec kidnap him
b) He is the key
c) A strange storm

2 *Multiple Choice:*
What is the control centre of the computer called?'
a) The Motherboard **1pt**
b) The Codec
c) Trojan

3 What is the name of the person who helps Trent? **2pts**

4 *Fill in the sentence:*
I just need the _____ so I can escape **3pts** this cursed computer.

5 What is happening in the image below? **2pts**

6 *Multiple Choice:*
At the end, why do you think Trent is not yet safe? **1pt**
a) The computer contains a virus
b) One of the Codec has escaped the game
c) The storm is still going

Answers on the next page. Every correct answer earns points (pts) Which level are you?

Level:
0 - 1pts = Trainee
2 - 4pts = Novice
5 - 7pts = Adept
8 - 9pts = Expert
10pts = Grand Master

Level Up Answers

1=(c), 2=(a), 3=Iris, 4= key,
5= Trent is using the key to open the Motherboard,
6=(b)

Explore...

Think about what happens next.

- How do you think Trent feels at the end of the story?

- If a Codec escaped, what would happen? How would Trent react?

- Who might help Trent get rid of the escaped Codec?

Other Titles

GRAFFIX BOOKS
OUT OF LINE
BY ALEX FRANCIS
ILLUSTRATED BY ALAN BROWN

#1
GRAFFIX BOOKS
HELIX: Into the Unknown
BY JAMIE HEX
ILLUSTRATED BY JAKE HILL

#2
GRAFFIX BOOKS
HELIX: First Encounter
BY JAMIE HEX
ILLUSTRATED BY JAKE HILL

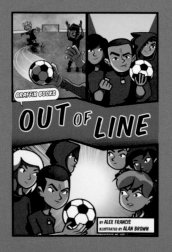

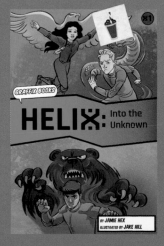

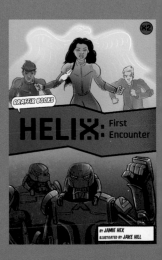